NOT EVERYONE'S DIALECT - STRINGS OF HEART

YOGITA LODHA

Contents

Contents

Preface

Not Everyone's Dialect - Strings of Heart is an elegant, unsettling poetry collection that's concerned with the significance of everyday words, meanings, and forms. Poems include images from nature, domestic scenes, faraway places, the woman and her environment, true bitter realizations and deep human emotions, relations, and love.

The book revolves around the sensational topics of women's empowerment, double standards existing in society, the various taboos of society, and also around love as a beautiful emotion. India has really been a very progressive country yet sometimes, somewhere we notice that the freedom to speak, express views & thoughts, conducting activities, are different for men & women. A man can speak up his mind; make his own decisions in life whereas a woman has limitation on her imagination as well. In a country where gods, that are worshipped are female idols & in the same country 1 out of 3 women has experienced physical or sexual violence at least once in a lifetime and this appears to be a big shame. Well, I am not here to be the feminist who supports only a particular gender or the part of the society and this has been well portrayed with the topics exhibiting the double standards against men too.

The other part of the book is soft and has an emotional touch as it revolves around love, attachments, fondness, tenderness, intimacy, warmth, and adoration. Love has many meanings. It can mean being affectionate towards a person, and the affection reciprocated. Love is a set of emotions that we experience. Love could also mean beliefs or behaviors that show your affection towards someone. Love is a feeling that everybody yearns for. It makes them feel happy and vital.

This book is a collection of poems that were all written in the time span of around 15 days of my covid quarantined period and every single one of them has been looked over, edited, and polished regularly up until its release. I've tried my best to make the things I'm saying in this book as clear, yet as interesting & nuanced as I possibly can. I hope that when you read this book, you feel the same things I did when I wrote it - excitement, wonder & joy. All in all, I hold this book and its poems very closely to my heart. I'm extremely proud & impressed with what I've done here, and I hope you are too.

Yogita Lodha (YoLo)

Acknowledgements

The world is a better place, thanks to people who want to develop and lead others. What make it even better are the people who share the gift of their time with the others. Thank you to everyone who strives to grow and help others to grow.

First and foremost, praises and thanks to God, the Almighty, for he showered his blessings throughout my writing work to complete it successfully.

Writing a book is harder than I thought and more rewarding than I could have ever imagined. None of this would have been possible without my parents, my mom **Madhu Lodha** and my dad **Sharad Lodha**. They taught me discipline, love, manners, respect, and so much more that has helped me succeed in life. I truly have no idea where I'd be if they hadn't given me support. I am extremely grateful to them for their love, prayers, care, and all their sacrifices. I hope my books and writings are something that I've done in my life to make you both proud.

To my little brother, **Akshat**, and sister, **Labdhi**, thank you for letting me know that you had nothing but great memories of me. So thankful to have you back in my life and enormous amount of gratitude for all your love, understanding, prayers, and continuing support during my writing period and pushing me when I am ready to give up.

I'm eternally grateful to my Friends **Pranjal Jain, Kaushal Thakkar, Labdhi Jain, Hardik Bothra, Aastha Batavia,** who has been helping me with the ideas over various topics all the while from deciding the coverage designs, colors, proofreads to the majors like discussing the subject topics and the ideas of the titles. I can barely find the words to express all the wisdom, love, and support you all gave me. Thanks for not just believing, but knowing that I could do this! I love you all always & forever!

Deepest thanks to my many patient, generous, and helpful readers.

A Word To Readers

As I write my way through life, one thing is evident, this heart is not one of gold; no, I am not pure. I am human. My work reflects the wistfulness and frustration that comes with merely being alive. I believe others may relate to it, but they'll have to read on to find out. No matter how much you relate to one of them, know that Poetry in itself is music to the eyes and it was always meant to be felt and forgotten.

Poetry in young India has been wildly popular and the trend apart from romance novels, chick-lits and rom-com has been observed in the short forms of writing too. As the written art evolves, Not Everyone's Dialect is to explore this format and aims to inspire more such poets to express themselves freely. All the poems were crafted from incidents that lasted like poetry itself- temporarily.

This poetry book might just have some poems that you read and get etched in your minds but you then have a hard time figuring out from which poetry book or poet it actually was from. **Still, I deeply urge and excitingly wait for your honest review and opinion over the suitable platform!**

Happy Reading!

"WINGS OF WOMEN"

Until You Spread Your Wings, You'll Have No Idea How High You Can Fly.

1. Being Woman

Blessed & cursed, my life's a struggle;
Be the era today or Mughals;
Unhinged & untamed, I have no master;
Men's behavior towards me is a disaster.

You call me weak, you call me a witch;
You subdue my speech and treat me like a bitch;
I am all of those & so much more;
To your feet I am floor;
To your house I am Door;
To your sea I am shore;
I am Everything you just can't ignore.

You burn me, you rape me, you kill me;
All just for being me;
I rise from the dead every single time;
And henceforth now I challenge every single crime;
With a new face, a new scent, I fight;
I love & I live to be free, I want to be light;
I am freedom's face!

I am the Men's Base!

Why Does He Feed On My Tears?

You fear my voice, you fear my fire;
I meant to be fly higher and higher;
I am strong but unlike you, kind;
But thing is, my love towards you is blind.

I show you what beauty truly is!
Let me have wings and bliss!
Oh you men! I am your shield;

For I cry, I am not here to be peeled;
I am your daughter, I am your wife
I am your mother, I gave you life
I am the Goddess!
I am Goodness
Lower your eyes!
Be bit humanize
I am a WOMAN!
I am a HUMANE!

<u>**Glossary**</u> -
Unhinged - mentally unbalanced; Untamed - Wild; **Subdue** - quieted, or bring under control; **Henceforth** - In the Future.

2. It's Always too Short, It's Always too revealing

Our Lives were in Peril,
Since the day we were born,
Because every time the clothes bought to wore,
Were always too short and too revealing.

A bunch of people disrespects me,
For wearing clothes above the knee,
Why would they make shorts that we should not wear,
because we get raped even in Burkhas at anytime and anywhere?

❧❧❧

She is judged to look so pretty and lean,
Is she not even allowed to be comfortable in her own skin?
She is told that she must have led him on given him the impression
Do they know she gave up her body for her life to get a concession?

You keep us locked at home and yet we're still not safe,
Still raped and they don't let us escape.
Her mind filled with confusion, and his filled with lust.
He took another part of her with each and every thrust.

She becomes deaf to the whistles and blind to the lewdness,
For her Stare her to be in absolute Nudeness,
Her consent didn't matter to him,
Her shrieks and pleas further fueled his vim.

Was being in my own skin a mistake?

His acts put her in great torment,
He Lives her to die, filling his heart with barbarous content.
She bleeds with all hurt and hate,

She Dies Every day taking all this as her fate

No one is spared,
Everyone they gaze and Everyone they glare,
Be it Little girl frock and pinafore,
Or the Saree, Burkha, Skirt you wore.

Your eyes just gleam
On listening to our muffled screams,
It Ain't about our clothes or sexuality,
But it's all your brutal and toxic mentality.

Glossary -
Peril - Risk; **Lean** - Perfect; **Impression** - Signaled; **Concession** – Compromise; **Thrust** – Poke and Push; **Lewdness** - involving or being sexual conduct that is considered indecent or offensive; **Shrieks** – Scream; **Pleas** – Plead; **Vim** – Enthusiasm; **Torment** - Severe physical or mental suffering; **Barbarous** - Extremely brutal; **Fate** - Destiny; **Gaze and Glare** - Stare intently; **Pinafore** - A collarless sleeveless dress worn over a blouse or jumper or shirt basically part of school uniform; **Gleam** – Shine with happiness; **Muffled** - Not loud because of being obstructed in some way by hand.

3. Scars Are Beautiful

One For the Acid Attack Survivors.

People call me nasty and kids are scared of me,
With Lots of sorrow and pity they see.
I have deep scars all over my body and face,
Which any cream or lotion can't replace.

When I look at my old pics I am not able to recognize myself,
But today I feel horrible about looking thyself.
I looked normal as any other girl,
As charming and not less than a Pearl.

It takes 2 minutes to put blush but only 2 seconds to scar a face.

These scars and this pain is the result of my saying no to a man who wanted to own me,
So He left me with pain and agony of the highest degree.
Should I regret saying no to that man double my age?
Modern-day devil disguised as sage.

Should I regret being a girl?
Or should I allow them to Hurl?
Should I believe the world which calls me ugly?
Or should I believe myself and say I am Lovely?

Yes, I don't regret anything, I don't think that I am ugly!

It's a Matter of your choice if you now deal with me roughly.
I have a beautiful loving heart and a forgiving soul,
To attain peace, to forget all foul.

I forgive the man who caused me this pain and I forgive those who want to make me feel ugly not because they deserve forgiveness but because I deserve my peace of mind!
Forgiving to forget the day because horror it reminds!
I am beautiful and no one can make me feel ugly…
I am beautiful enough so that you can freely hug me...
I love myself and feel proud to be who I am- a woman, a wonderful woman!
A someone not defined by a man!

<u>Glossary</u> -
Nasty – Ugly; **Pity** – Regret; **Pearl** - a person or thing of great rarity and worth; **Disguise** - Conceal one's identity; **Hurl** – Throw with great force; **Foul**- Evil

4. Double Standards

We want our daughters to convince their husbands to leave their parent's house,
But then we call our daughters-in-law witches and blood-sucking louse.
We are okay with our daughters earning more than their husbands,
but force daughters-in-law to take up lesser paying jobs to boost son's ego up and end.
We think it is the duty of the girl to look after the parents on the Inlaws side,
but Why can't a boy too same abide.

We march and light candles and we abuse rapists,
but refuse to let our sons marry rape victims and become their therapists.
We want virgin daughters-in-law,
but our sons can have fun and break any law.
One is forbidden to share, meet or talk to strangers,
but it is perfectly fine to get married and be expected to sleep with one, and surprisingly it's not considered a danger.

I See and Make Standards

Girls expect guys to foot their bill,
and then call themselves feminists of free will.
It is okay for a girl to lash out at guys when they cut through lines,
but when they do the same, the guy should allow them to do so silently and say it's all fine?
In India, it's always shown women are being ill-treated,
How the woman is the only one who could be cheated?

It is okay for guys to wreck a place,
But it's a woman's job to keep it clean and make it a

palace.
A woman who's a good cook is compared to a goddess,
and a man with the same talent is questioned about his masculinity and its ignorance of his goodness.
It is okay for a woman to be sensitive and be emotionally high,
but men are not even supposed to cry.

It is okay to piss on the road,
but kissing is illegal and shame is showed.
A woman should be waxed and plucked and considered fair,
While a man is admired for being a hairy bear.
A waxed man is ridiculed and is bombed,
But a waxed woman is a norm.

A girl is asking for it when she is raped and that news is aflame,
so what did the guy do when he is subjected to the same?
Oh wait, we don't think guys are raped and molest,
We see them only as of the figure that protects.
Stay at home moms are tigresses,
But stay-at-home dads are sissies.

The guy should propose with a diamond ring,
While the girl should not do anything,
Because hey, girls don't propose,
To plunk their hard-earned salaries is what guys are to supposed.
We oppose dowry because ultimately we fear the police,
But give expensive 'gifts' as a token to ensure peace.

Stand for rights of any other religion and you are secular,
But all Hindus are still communists and this is regular.
All the while trying to prove which religion is the best,
We end up killing each other and just protest.
And yet all the blood that flows is always red.
How are we different then?

We trust our neighbors to decide what marks our kid should get,
but when our kid tries to commit suicide, we try to hide the same from them, and that's so sad.
We love our sons even when they throw us out,
And yet the daughter who welcomes us into her home is a burden to us and we shout.
It is okay if our son or daughter has some faults and they should be accepted,

But the same doesn't apply to anybody else and we make sure that they are repented.
These double standards have got no end,
The entire book may fall short to comprehend..

Glossary –
Louse – Insect that sucks blood; **Ridiculed** – Mocked; **Aflame** – On Fire; **Repented** - Feel or express sincere regret or remorse about one's wrongdoing or sin; **Comprehend** – Include.

5. MoM

She is the sunlight in your day.
She is the moon you see far away.
She is the tree for you to lean upon.
She is the one that makes troubles be gone.

She is the one who taught you about life,
How not to fight and what is right.
She is the words inside your song.
She is your love, your life, your mom.

She is the one who knows you best,
When it's time to learn and time to rest.
She is the one who has helped you to chase your dream.
She hears your heart and your screams.

Selfless Love

She is the one who always care.
Whose soul is pure, whose love is rare.
She is the one who is always there,
When scared of ghost,
Or the way is lost.

She is the one who always pray.
When you are ill,
Or on the top of the hill for your thrill.

Afraid of life but looking for love.
You are blessed, for almighty sent her from above.
Hold her tight and hug her.
And millions of times you thank her.

Glossary –

Lean Upon - To Show Trust; **Almighty** - God

6. Mother Earth - Awkward Conversation

Stripped and scorched and choked and abused,
Peeled and poisoned and plundered and misused,
Pillaged and robbed and burned and Murdered by degrees,
We all are cruel human beings, and we need to agree.

Bound to her by gravity, she being part of us,
Formed from the same clay, she is our mother thus,
Lungs take in her breath, her ocean runs within our veins,
We depend on her, be it green fertile plains or good rains.

I asked Mother Earth, why are you looking so sticky,
Let me know your problems, and I shall help out quickly,
Said she if you could recycle… That's easy to do,
But insane I, too busy to recycle, wish I could help you.

She pleaded for nontoxic fertilizers to be used in the yard,
I apologized, for it's too hard,
She suggested organic food and electric car,
But poor me, I have to travel so far.

Save Me, My Child!

Said she while groaning in pain,
Why Humans have turned out to be disdain,
She marked that she was once a paradise, all lush and green,
now decaying and rotting and it's a horrible sight to be

seen.

She is sobbing and we need to save her,
as we have to live here, for years and years,
We have to stop using plastic, we need to purify the air,
Can get rid of landfills and show her that we care.
The earth is our paradise; we need to care for it more,
Then and only then Mother Earth will not cry anymore.

Glossary –

Stripped – Remove all Coverings; **Scorched** – Burn by flames or heat; **Choked** – Have severe difficulty in breathing because of a constricted or obstructed throat or a lack of air; **Peeled** – Remove Skin; **Plundered** – To Rob; **Pillaged** – Using Violence; **Groaning** – Sound Conveying pain; **Disdain** - The feeling that someone or something is unworthy of one's consideration or respect; **Paradise** - Heaven

7. UnMan Yourself

Let's Hear from Sandeep today!

Greetings here to everyone, its Sandeep,
And Society Gawk at me as I weep.
I found it hard when they snatched my Doll,
And laid the rules that boys are meant for bats and ball.
As a kid, I once cried in public and everyone giggled,
Appears as if they found lip-smacking fun with pickles.
The little me wiped my eyes,
with smiling faces, face full of lies.
Young and tender me finds is hard to understand,
Why I can not cry...for just because I am a Men.

I Just Shout,
All Aloud,
Normalize the society where the men cry out his heart,
Normalize him showing emotions when someone leaves and go apart,
Normalize his tears if he wins or even when he lose,
Normalize even when he fells out due to untied shoes,

For you might have not heard about my friend Kevin and his cry,
When Kevin failed in fifth grade, his father said work hard, be a boy, don't cry,
When Kevin's mother left him. People asked him to be a strength to family and not to cry,
When Kevin's girlfriend left him, his friends said, be a dude, for a girl you can't cry,
When Kevin lost his job, his wife said common men work harder, don't cry,
When Kevin committed suicide, he wondered who would cry.

If I raise hand and be K@bir S!ngh, the bunch of feminists appears,
They Blaze and fires and heat up the matter of misogyny;
But when the delivery boy gets hit, all vanish and disappear,
Because he was a man and the things weren't worth attention any;
If I be K@bir B@nsal "Ka" and performs household works in variety,
Patriarchal traditions unfollowed, Mocks my society.
If I be K@bir Deewan of znmd , say yes to marriage even without intention,
Fearing the yelling of my girl and wild societal

contravention.
I think something has gone wrong with the name Kabir,
Or is it just that in the end, it is the man who gets a stir.

I was always told a man is somebody who hides his countenance adeptly,
One who behaves erectly and correctly,
But what exactly defines a man?
Is he meant only to be the head of the clan?
Is it the hair on the cheeks?
Or the one who flaunts the abs six?
Or the depth of their pockets?
Or the ability to buy a locket?
Or is it the strength of our arms?
Or the one with all powers and charms?

Hardened by my life's journey making restless soul,
All my emotions packed tight into an endless hole.
Even let me wet my pillow at times,
Without fearing the society and fake to look all fine.
But Alas! I the product of the system where expressing myself is a sin,
I have to bury them all inside and look alive and have to carry all my kin.
A deep urge to stop slaying,
Couldn't end up saying.
Mard Ko Dard Nahi Hota!
Kyu Mard Inssan Nahi Hota?

Glossary -

Gawk – Stare; **Lip Smacking** – Very Tasty; **Misogyny**- prejudice/ Violence against women; **Countenance** – a person's facial expression; **Stir** – irritation; **Adeptly** – Skillfully; **Erectly** - upright or straight. **Clan** – Family/tribe; **Patriarchy** – A Society with male authority; **Kin** – Maintaining Relations

English Translation - " Mard Ko Dard Nahi Hota, Kyu Mard Insaan Nahi Hota - Men doesn't feel pain, why is he not Human?

8. My Versions

For so many years, all my life,
I've been so many different versions of myself,
I've been an unrelenting, angry, madness tearing/
ripping/screaming/shredding. pulling myself apart at all
my edges.

I've been a hurricane of melancholy,
swelling deep/pouring out/spilling over.
drowning myself every chance I could.

I've been a reckless endeavor of stubborn, impulsive/
unthinking/
reactive. trapping myself inside dangerous places.

all I've ever wanted was to be a version of myself I could be
proud of.
One that wasn't so heavy all the time.
One that was kinder, more thoughtful,
softer / lighter/gentler/easier/better

but that one never stays.

Which of me is Best?

Glossary –

Unrelenting – Uncompromising; **Ripping** – tear or pull (something) quickly or forcibly away from something or someone; **Shredding** – Chop Finely;
Hurricane - Storm; **Melancholy** – Feeling Sad; **Swelling deep/pouring out/spilling over** – Filling yourself with tears and then pouring it out later; **Reckless** – Careless; **endeavor** – Venture or trial; **Impulsive** – Spontaneous, without thinking;

9. MeN

Men scared of
The bold and fierce you
The complex and confused you
The Indecisive and Raging you
Don't deserve
The soft and sweet you
The tearful and vulnerable you
The wild and tender you

Glossary –
Raging– Violent; **Venerable** – One who need care

10. Rose and Thorns

The world thought she was a nest of roses.
But she also came with thorns.
As gentle as a fragrant breeze she was
But was also like a vicious storm.
She didn't need the safety of men,
Her thorns protected her well.
She loved the one she cared for,
For the rest, she was the living hell.

11. A Tale Of Bravery

A night of discomfort, Ends at four in the morning.
With an aching gut,
My period arrives, without any warning.
Forcing myself to sacrifice my sleep,
With groggy eyes and blurry vision,
Heading towards the supplies where I keep,
Like a zombie walking, resulting in a collision.

Band aiding myself,
Stopping the flood of blood.
Shrinking to the size of an elf,
I lie down in my bed, with a thud.
The sun rises,
And so the pain.
Dealing with the sleep crisis,
Also worrying about the stain.

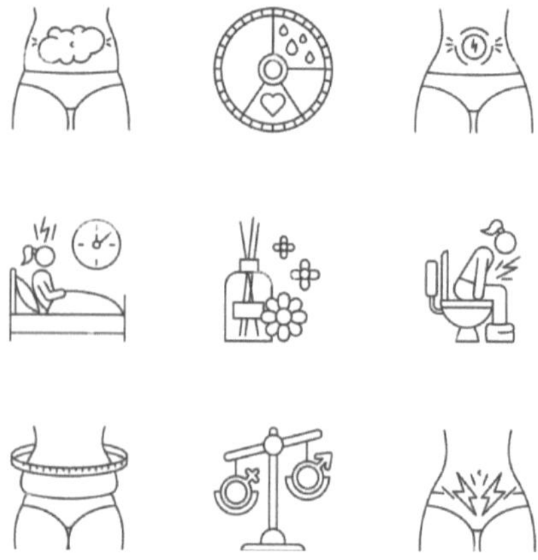

Winning the battle, and mastering.

It's just the beginning,
It'll get much worse.
The mood swings and the bleeding,
Argh! It's a curse.
For the next couple of days,
I'll be acting cool,
But will be lost in the inner maze,
And drowning in the red pool.

The pills and the pads are my pals for now.
The cravings will make me go nuts.
Don't let me raise my brow,
Just serve me, without ifs and buts.

The feeling of being ripped apart,
And the misery all I bear,
Will make me stronger by heart.

A tale of bravery, I'd like to share.
It's like, a child is sent to war,
Who needs love and pampering.
Growing into a woman, I roar,
Winning the battle, and mastering.

Glossary -

Aching – Paining; **Groggy** - weak, or unsteady, especially from illness, intoxication, sleep; **Elf**- a supernatural creature of folk tales, typically represented as a small, delicate, elusive figure in human form with pointed ears, magical powers, and a capricious nature; **Maze** - puzzle through which one has to find a way.

12. Be Skinny But Not Too Skinny

They say be skinny but not too skinny.
They also remark not to be pooh the Winnie
They say be girly and ladylike, for that is pretty.
Or they also give their so-called views on the curves of deity
They say be curvy but only in the right places.
They say always carry a smile on your faces.

Who made such rules?
Those were the fools from learned schools
Who were these people so cruel?
Who gave them the authority of approval?
Why can't I just be me?
Be it a zero size or figure three.

Slowly in my head, the truth starts to creep,
Why were their thoughts so down and cheap.
They too were never accepted for who they were.

Because nobody for them applauded or cheer
They too were shamed for every freckle, every curve.
They too were observed thus building mentality of reserve

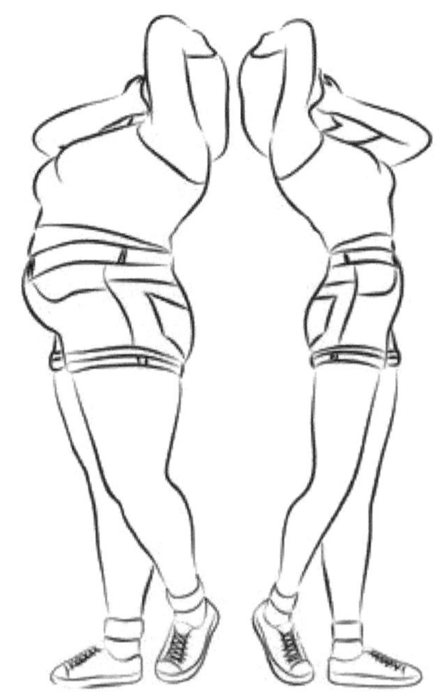

Don't let your size hinder yourself.

It is not their fault entirely, now I see,
Society spares no one, no one is free.
They just don't want us to face the hate they had to feel,
So they just suggest having a little amount of meal.

In the process of getting the world to like us though, we started hating our own bodies,
So we just start doing everything to ensure no tease.

Taught to be somebody's instead of somebodies,
Making us swing between the thin bodies and the fat bodies.
Is it alright that they won't let us be ourselves?
Shouldn't they know better since they've been through it themselves?
The world before them changed them, got into their head.
But we must not give in, or the real us will be dead.

Glossary -

Winnie – A Bear Cartoon character who is fat; **Deity** – Statue of Goddess; **Freckle** - patch of light brown color on the skin.

"LOVE - A BEAUTIFUL EMOTION"

What's Meant To Be, Will Always Find His Way.

13. My Love till Eternity

Hope to see you some day
waiting for me,
With a spark in your eyes
And a smile on your lips.
Beyond the lush greens and bright meadow
On a deserted barren land
Where I can be with you,
Just you
And tweak my soft palm in your hand;

Hope to see you some day....
With a glint in your eyes; unmistakable
Laden with love
That's just for me....
Flowing endlessly like a up tide,
In all its might
And your fingers stroking,
the blushed cheeks
Tinted red with ecstasy;

Hope to see you some day!

Hope to see you some day....
humming a song of our love;
That soothes my withered soul,
Weaved in a fervent melody;
And whilst your eyes dance
With a mischief
You turn a little greedy.
To Have Little more of me
A little wild of me.

And I hope;
That someday.....Comes soon......
As the summers depart; longing for the chilled winter;
And before the winters' turns glacial,

Hope to see you march upon like spring
In all its breezy verve,
A little chirpier, a little more special .

And when that someday shall come......
You shall be mine..
Forever....
Till eternity!

Glossary -

Lush – Dark; **Meadow** – Grassland; **Tweak** – Move; Glint – Shine; Laden – Filled; Ecstasy – Bliss; Withered – Dry; Fervent – Passionate; Whilst – at the same time.

14. My Man In Uniform!

She has no desires to love the uniform and be proud;
For her the chime of his calmness & charmness was more loud.
She want to serve that person and his family,
Who had courage to die for the nation happily.

Always she needed a man who is loving,
The one who acknowledges her emotions without saying.
Whensoever's she thinks about him & thought he is perfect,
She loves him thoroughly & without any expect.

She loves him because of his notion and heart;
She is in love with him not with his pride profession and when he departs.

My Man In Uniform.

Whenever he for serving the nation and on for wars,
Her breaths are so heavy that they goes far and far.

She always carve for his company and burn in loneliness,
But she fights her sorrow, she acts like a lioness.
She always pray for his long and safe life,
Because she knows her worth as a warrior's wife.

Sometimes she is on cloud nine looking at the stars on his shoulder,
But she more wishes to together become older.
Yes, in love with the man in uniform;
No not his uniform, but only the man in form.

Glossary -

Chime – Sound; **Notions** – Beliefs;

15. I Am Learning to be Okay!

I am learning, to be okay,
When people walk away.
Accepting, they have a part to play,
And not everyone's meant to stay.

I am learning, to walk alone
And not seek comfort in their embrace,
To speak of my thoughts freely
And accept rejection with grace.

I am learning, to hold back
And not put my heart out to be played,
For they would have made the effort
If it meant more than they displayed.

And Yes! I Am Okay !

I am still learning, how to care properly.
Cause people have some twisted ways,
Realizing it's not all its made out to be,
Extra efforts often ends in disappointments and heartbreaks.

Glossary -

Embrace – Hug/ here presence; **Notions** – Beliefs;

16. Dear Love

Dear Love!
I'm a candle in a day light,
While sun is shining in the blue sky,
But still you love the candle.
I'm a little star in a night,
When full moon is in the sky,
But still you love the star.
I'm a tiny wild flower on the grass,
Surrounded by orchids in a forest,
But still you love the tiny flower.

Dear love!
Thank for all the love you bestow upon me.
You are the diamond, In the beautiful ring of your hand,
And i love that diamond embedded in your heart.
You are the calm and alluring sea,
Merging all the rivers in yourself,
And I am in love with your depth.
You are the aesthetic moon,
With all the stars around,
I being one of them,
And I am in love with your inner moon-like beauty.

Glossary -

Orchids – Symbolizes thoughtfulness, refinement, fertility, beauty, charm, and love; **Alluring** – Very Attractive;

17. Lost Love

Erstwhile I unlatched my feelings to you,
The feelings were not new and had grew,
But you wanted me to be your gem, just as a best friend,
And that made me feel like dying to the very end.

I was learning the meaning of life and lime,
When fascination smack me for the first time,
I was deeply into it thinking that it's a true feeling,
But that wasn't, it hurts and was not healing.

It all ignited with just a hello,
And now my spirit won't let you go,
A tremendous battle ignited in my heart that day,
Can't comprehend what it wanted to say.

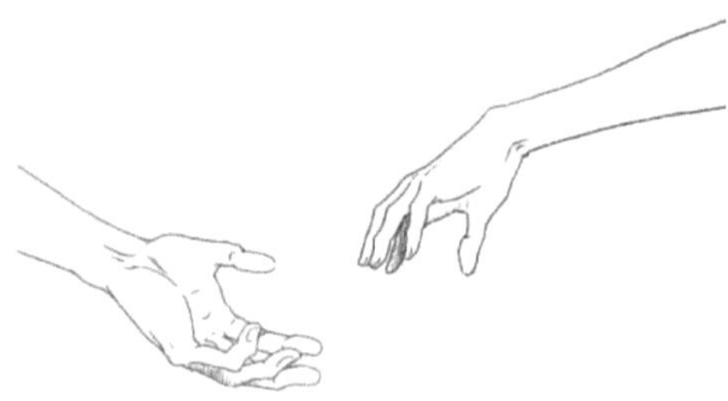

You buried me with your every manly look,
My brain froze and my knees shook,
I always wanted more and more,
But alas, my presence for you, bore!

There were the days where I dreamed you and me,
And even today it's still you that I see,
I felt that if those sweet dreams turn into reality,
My affection would have lasted till eternity.

It's now difficult to respire without you,
And even much burdensome to find any new,

It feels like a suffocating dove.
The way I loved, I wished, you too have loved.

I did whatnot, but went unnoticed,
And in consideration, got "No" from his notice,
I know to love is not to barter,
But I lost you, I lost my laughter.

I vanished myself for him while putting all efforts,
But in end, it was me who was hurt,
I had the fire of Phoenix in my eyes,
But after him, I turned cold, pale, and lost all my wise.

Those movies, food, and outings leveled up the hormone,
Made me do all follies and I acted much of a Moron,
But this was a period that helped me to discover the truth,
Love does nothing but spoil your time, energy, and youth.

Days passed, months passed, years passed I worked on myself,
I healed from a wound I got in my life for myself,
Guard your heart and spirit and soul and mind,
Unless you want yourself in a disruptive bind.

So the story ends here
and it has been fulfilling,
I would miss you terribly,
But I leave you lovingly...

<u>**Glossary**</u> -

Erstwhile – One day/before; **Unlatched** – reveal; **Smack** – Hit; **Ignited** - arouse; **Comprehend** – Decode; **Phoenix** - a person or thing regarded as uniquely remarkable in some respect.

18. Before the Dusk

I'll miss you.
You will miss the moments.
The moments will remember,
It was beautiful before dusk.

But darkness is a certainty.
This system is a necessity.
Our crime was forgiven.
The forgiveness, unforgiving.

Unraveled truth,
This far we have come.
Can we back down?
It's the question least done.

T'was Beautiful Before the Dusk

Coffee by the side,
And a caffeinated life.
Sequencing the truth,
While comprehending lies.

Why do we ache?
For what's not of our share.
What we left where,
Was meant to be there.

We had reasons to cling,
But the parting was what we chose.
We oxidized a fire,
Without preparing for the chaos.

Pretty much parted ways now,
And this loneliness is full of guts.
The moments will remember,
It was beautiful before the dusk.

<u>**Glossary**</u> -

Sequencing – Arranging; **Comprehending** – Analyzing;

19. Adore Me Still

I am spilt ink to the poetry
of your life,
I am chaos to the order
in your mind,
I'm the loud voice in the library
And the laughter at a funeral,
Can you find it in your heart
to adore me still?

20. Too Far Yet Too Close

You are so far,
Yet you are here.
I can't see you always,
But I can feel you near.

I can't touch you,
But I hold you close.
No matter where you are,
You reside here in my heart.

Wherever I go,
Your essence is alive
In me.
For I can't see your expressions,
But I can imagine
You laugh.

You are to be here,
For I wish to never let

The pearls to drop
From your shelly eyes.

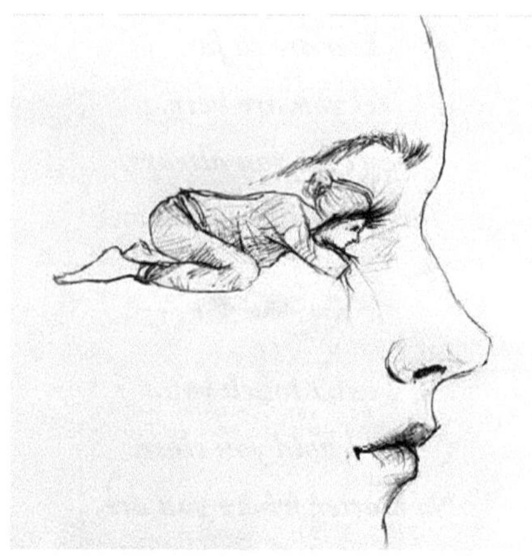

I Carry you wherever I go

All I wish is to be your life,
For you are my sorrow's knife.
And I believe,
You will be the one I will never leave.

Hopefully the lies between us
Will disappear soon,
Because all I want

Is To Be With You.

Miles apart,
yet so close.
The feel of you being alive in me.
Vanishes the distance.
The same way moon spreads
Light in the dark night sky.
The same way sun lights up
the world
And happiness fly.

Yes, my love
I wish to be your salvation,
And want you to be my creation.
And I wish you to spread light
Destroying away all my plights.
I wish to be your smile,
When you are tired with work's pile,
And I want to be your life,
And keep my promises,
Till the day my soul comprises me.
Till the day you are alive in me.

21. Dreams

I close my eyes
To reveal turquoise waters
Dissolving heaps of discontent
Caressing grains of sand

I close my eyes
To unearth a vibrant arboretum
Devoting space to growth
Leaving room for variation

I close my eyes
To visions of solitude:
Filling me with boundless ingenuity
Creating harmonious echoes of ease

I open my eyes
To present actualities
Longing for imaginary spaces
That dwell between light and dark

I close my eyes again
To return to my sacred sanctuary
Searching for a serenity
Found only in a dream.

Dreams are Better

Glossary -

Turquoise – Greenish Blue Color; Caressing – stroking gently or lovingly; **Unearth** - find (something) in the ground by digging; **Arboretum** - a botanical garden devoted to trees; **Ingenuity** - the quality of being clever; **Serenity** - the state of being calm

22. The Serene Love

He picked her up when she was broken.
He dried her tears, no words spoken.
He cared for her when she was weak.
He guarded her when she was in peril.
Unaware she was, she could calm his devils

If only he could find the words to speak,
He was too shy, for he never wanted his feeling to leak,
So he loved her implicitly, without being a freak.
She ignored him, for she had fears
That he might give her another bunch of tears.
Though she was wrong,
He held her strong.

She did not know when he took her heart,
With his gestures and his alluring art.
Moments became memories,
When feelings created treasuries.
Time took her to a modish world,
Where the dew drops were pearled.

She decided not to drain a chance,
For she craved to be the heroine
Of a story full of romance.
With a bunch of orchid,
A taxi she boarded.
He waited at the lakeside,
Waiting to get chided.
He turned around,
And got astound.

On her knees, with that bouquet,
She said," Hey you! will you be my partner in every way?"
'His modesty, her fragility,
A relationship with pure serenity.

Glossary -

Peril – Danger; **Implicitly** – Completely; **Alluring** – Very Attractive; **Modish** – Modern; **Orchid** – Kind Of Flower; **Chided** – Scold; **Astound** – Surprise; **Modesty** – Humility/ Kindness; **Fragility** – Weakness; **Serenity** – Calm

23. Emptiness

In empty spaces
In known faces
I see sadness all around
In crowded places
I can see the traces
Of pain muting the happy sound
The grief slyly braces
Until your heart ceases
To accept the love profound
The lesson surfaces
In tiny phrases
That grief is always around

Don't fight
Let it stay,
The more you challenge it
It will somehow find its way

Accept it
Respect it
Let the gloom linger for a day
And when you don't expect it
Your grief will wither away.

<u>Glossary</u> -

Slyly – In Cunning Manner; **Braces** – Support; **Linger** - Stay in a place longer than necessary because of a reluctant to leave; **Wither** – Fade away.

24. If A Writer Falls In Love

If A Writer Falls In Love With You,
You Are One Among The Million And Lucky Too.
You're Special,
Because For Her, You Need Not Even Wrestle.
From The Moment You Steal Her Heart,
She Comes Out With All Alluring Art.

You'll Become The Reason For The Words That Fill Her Pages,
You Become Her Metaphor, And All Images.
She Will Write About The Child In You,
She Will Rhyme Everything That No One Even Knew.
She Will Describe You In The Most Beautiful Creative Ways..
That You Won't Have Even The Words To Say

A Fuel To My Pen

Everyone Who Reads Will Wish That They Were You
And Would Wish To Be Rhymed Just Like You Were Put Through
& When You Die, You're Always Alive In Her Poetry,
Man! She Just Makes You An Evergreen Tree.

About The Author

Yogita Lodha is Ahmedabad based writer and poet. She loves writing short topics and creating rhymes.

By her profession she talks about, Finance, tax, auditing, and accounting.

By her passion she talks about, Poems, Alliterations, stories, Short Contents & Thoughts.

As a writer, she is a free bird. She won't have a specific topic which is the only one she writes about, she does answer what she likes to, what she believes in, not to "please" someone and fake it out. She believes in extremes.

She is a gender-neutral writer as well, and don't take a particular side till some question that makes no sense pointing someone comes up.

She is also an author of the book "Not Everyone's Dialect- A Collection of Alliterations"- an elegant, unsettling poetry collection that's concerned with the significance of everyday words, meanings, images from nature, domestic scenes, faraway places, and human emotions. She is also a co-author in two other books.

As a Human, She believes in the "Infinite Loop ∞ of Observing, Learning & Delivering."

Thank-you Readers

Dear Reader,

Let me ask you something — who is the writer without their readers? It is an eternal question — would art exist without spectator? I don't know the answer. But I know that every time I write — I write with my readers in mind.

Readers are the writer's mirror — in you, we see the reflection of our words and ideas. You help us to shape them, translate thoughts into sentences and communicate them with you.

Knowing that there are people who are genuinely interested in the ideas that we share makes it a whole more interesting. It creates a space for conversation - writing is not a monologue.

It's an indescribable feeling to know that you've touched someone's life, maybe changed it a bit or just gave them a reminder of a thing that they've already known.

Writing makes us friends with the people that we've never met and probably never will. It connects and unites us no matter where we are and who we are.

So thank you, dear reader!

Thank you for taking the time to read my poetrics.

Thank you for being the inspiration.

Thank you for your encouragement and kind words.

Thank you for sharing your points of view, especially when you don't agree.

Thank you for trusting me.

9 798886 064988

Printed by Libri Plureos GmbH in Hamburg, Germany